FEAR OF FLYING

How to Overcome Fear of Flying

GIUSEPPE FORMATO

Copyright © 2014 Giuseppe Formato

All rights reserved.

ISBN-10: 1533060800
ISBN-13: 978-1533060808

This information is protected by intellectual property laws, including trademark and copyright laws. Except as permitted under the Act (for example a fair dealing for the purposes of study, research, criticism, review or personal use) no part of this book may be reproduced or transmitted in any form or by any means, electronic or mechanical, including photocopying, recording, or by any information storage and retrieval system, without written permission from the author. Every effort has been made to trace and acknowledge copyright. The author apologies for any accidental infringement and welcomes information to redress the situation.

Disclaimer

The information is of a general nature and does not take into account your personal situation. The information presented is for educational purposes only. The author will not bear any responsibility or liability for any action taken by any person, persons or organization on the purported basis of the information contained in this book and any supporting material. References to other information, websites or events should not be understood as an endorsement of such information, website or events. Every effort has been made to ensure that this book is free from errors or omissions. However, the author shall not accept responsibility for injury, loss or damage occasioned to any person acting or refraining from action as a result of material in this book whether or not such injury, loss or damage is in any way due to any negligent act or omission, breach of duty or default on the part of the author.

CONTENTS

Introduction

Your Journey to Freedom from Fear Begins 1

Defining Your Fears 3

Understanding the Symptoms 5

Set the Facts Straight 8

Conquering Your Fear 11

All or Nothing 21

Conclusion

INTRODUCTION

I want to thank you and congratulate you for purchasing this book, **"Fear of Flying"**.

This book contains proven steps and strategies on how to overcome your fear of flying for good.

For example, in this book you will discover the following strategies:

- How to use meditation in relaxing before your flight
- Why people fear flying in the first place
- Discover the symptoms of aviophobia
- Expert techniques before, during and after your flight
- The best teas to drink to calm you down before your flight
- And more!

Thanks again for purchasing this book, I hope you enjoy it!

YOUR JOURNEY TO FREEDOM FROM FEAR BEGINS

Ah yes, the dreaded, gut-wrenching, spine-tingling, heart-racing, mind-blowing and bone-crushing fear of flying!

This type of fear is one of the most common phobias; it ranks among the top-grossing all-time winning fears such as the fear of the dark and fear of spiders.

What's it with the fear of flying anyway?

Ask anyone with this kind of fear and you will get wild stories and ideas such as the fear of being inside a confined space, suffocating, the fear of crashing in mid-air with another plane, the fear of crashing into the ocean, the fear of being suspended in air with only a few inches of metal holding you and of course the fear of being thousands of meters above the ground.

All of these different kinds of fears basically make up the fear of flying and discovering some effective ways to handle all these fears will be the subject of this book.

Is your fear of flying holding you back?

Have you ever turned down an amazing vacation overseas just because of this fear?

Is your career on a standstill because you cannot fly abroad?

Are you forced to live where you are while your family has migrated overseas because of your fear?

If you said yes to any of these then it is time to finally get hold of your life and start conquering your fear!

There is no time to waste!

Your journey to the new you begins today!

DEFINING YOUR FEARS

What is fear of flying?

Before anything else, let's discover what fear of flying is all about.

Experts say that the best way to conquer any kind of fear is to face it and by facing your fear means learning what the fear of flying is, what causes it, what are the known symptoms and of course finding out ways to conquer your fear.

Aviophobia is fear of flying or flying in general.

People who have aviophobia state that their fears of flying range from the actual flight to a number of different fears.

It is actually a combination of fears rolled into one.

It is the fear of being in a confined space, moving across the skies, travelling across oceans and cities with just a few inches of metal to cover you! But regardless of what people with aviophobia call their fear or describe what they feel, the fear of flying is real AND it can be overcome.

Realizing your fears

If you are unsure of what you are feeling or what you feel about flying, you may not be totally convinced that you have aviophobia in the first place.

To overcome your fears, you need to realize and to accept that you are indeed anxious and fearful and afterwards you can create a suitable management plan to control what you are feeling.
.

UNDERSTANDING THE SYMPTOMS

What are the 7 common symptoms of aviophobia?

1. There is an overwhelming feeling of anxiety and fear. Just the mere thought of flying increases your heart beat and makes you very uneasy. Remember, it is just the actual thought of the act; you are not flying or going to fly soon. The feeling is also evident when you watch movies about flying, crashing or an actor being in a plane.

2. There are physical symptoms too such as increased heart beat, increased respiration or you are suddenly out of breath, increased blood pressure, headaches, pain on any part of the body, stomach cramps, nausea, vomiting and so on.

3. Some people may shake, feel weak, lose focus, become very confused and very irritable when they are about to board a plane.

4. Some may feel restless and may suffer from sleeplessness days before their scheduled flight.

5. Some may suffer from changes in appetite, weight loss or weight gain, changes in physical activity and depression.

6. Some may experience episodes of panic especially days or hours before boarding a flight. Signs of panic could range from shaking to screaming, from crying to breaking down.

7. Some may remove themselves from reality or become withdrawn

from the fact that they are experiencing fear. They would appear to be OK but soon would exhibit outrageous symptoms such as crying, panic and poor perception of reality.

All these symptoms should be detected as early as possible to be able to address fears of flying.

Some say that it is natural for anyone to have some form of fear especially when flying for the first time and this could be true for young children to adults.

But having profound symptoms could be dangerous especially being unable to control panic and anxiety.

Is fear of flying normal?

As mentioned a while ago, the fear of flying could be a normal experience especially for someone that has never flown before.

However this fear becomes an irrational fear when a person exhibits profound symptoms such as severe panic, crying and withdrawal.

Anyone that has these symptoms could be at risk of injuring himself or others!
Aside from flying for the first time, here are some common reasons why people have aviophobia:

- Any kind of troublesome experience while flying before may still affect you today. You may have suffered from turbulence while on air, an actual crash, a hijacking in midair, a violent thunderstorm, an engine failure and so on.

- Any news about past or recent mishaps in the air may have also stirred your fear.

- A movie that you saw may have triggered your fear of flying.

- A personal experience of someone close to you or a friend may also affect you.

- A weather report could also cause some fear.

- Experiencing an actual outburst of fear of flying such as actual panic, crying and screaming before or during a flight could also cause fear.

- Believing in myths and stories about flying could also cause fear.

Realizing your symptoms

Now that you have read all the possible symptoms and reasons why people fear flying, you will now be able to pinpoint your own symptoms and do something about it.

You may be new to flying and just experiencing these for the first time or you have been dreading flying and have had these symptoms for a long time; no matter how simple or how profound your symptoms are, you can do something to reduce, if not remove your fear of flying completely.

SET THE FACTS STRAIGHT

A glance at the statistics

Let the National Safety Council provide you with statistics of how likely you will die in an airplane accident compared to other mishaps. Here is a table of the latest odds:

Cause of Death	Annual Number Lifetime of Deaths / Odds
Heart Disease	631,636/ 1 in 6
Cancer	562,875/ 1 in 7
Heavy Drinking	79,000/ 1 in 49
Fall Accidents	22,631/ 1 in 171
Car Accidents	12,772/ 1 in 303
Pedestrian Accidents	5,958/ 1 in 649
Motorcycle Accidents	5,024/ 1 in 770
Bicycle Accidents	820/ 1 in 4,717
Airplane Accidents	**550/ 1 in 7,032**
Lightning	46/ 1 in 84,079

Source: National Safety Council and Centers for Disease Control. The chart indicates odds of dying from a specific cause. The rates were calculated using the cause of death listed on U.S. death certificates in 2007. Lifetime odds are calculated by dividing the 2007 population (301,290,332) by the number of deaths (creating one-year odds of death), and then, dividing that figure by the life expectancy of a person born in 2007 (77.9 years).

Looking at the data presented above, your fear of dying in an airplane accident is incomparable with the odds of dying in other modes of transportation.

You are more likely to get hurt and possibly die a painful death if you ride a bike; drive a car and even simply walking down the street.

You are basically safer when you fly in a plane and this is simply because of the following reasons:

1. Commercial airline pilots and charter plane pilots undergo grueling hours of training and flight experience and are therefore the most efficient, reliable and the most professional in their field. Not only is your life in his hands but the airline pilot is responsible for all the passengers in an airline and that is a HUGE responsibility!

2. Airline companies have stricter rules regarding aircraft inspection and maintenance before these are allowed to fly. Experienced and professional aircraft technicians do periodic checks on aircrafts to ensure their safety.

3. Improved technologies have made flying safer over the years. This goes with technologies used in communication, on-board aircraft technologies, air traffic control technologies and safety technologies on the ground and in the air.

4. When safety and security are concerned, there are improved efforts in the detection and prevention of terrorist activities in airports and in aircrafts. Airports all over the world are use teams of security personnel to check baggage, people, aircraft and the perimeter of all suspicious activities.

5. Finally, flying a plane is safer and a lot faster. You will be able to get to where you want to go in just a few minutes which reduce your risks of other dangers while on the road.

So now that you have an idea of how safe it is to fly in an airplane, you may be ready to conquer your fear of flying.

A word of caution: *no one said that conquering your fear is easy.*

There are strategies that will push you to your limit and make you face your fears in the eye.

Conquering your aviophobia is taking steps to eventually free yourself from this fear for good!

If you are ready, then let the next chapter guide you in conquering your fear of flying for good.

CONQUERING YOUR FEAR

Overcoming your fear of flying

It would already be a given to use strategies BEFORE you actually ride an airplane however, a better way of dealing with aviophobia is to support the person from the start of his flight, during the flight and of course afterwards.

The following are a few effective ways to do these. Find out which one suit you best.

Before your flight

A large number of strategies to conquer aviophobia focus on how to do it before the actual flight.

Here are some very effective ones:

1. **Find out what to expect in an airplane flight.**

The more you know about your flight, the more you will be able to learn how to control your fears. People that are new to flying often feel fearful because they do not know what to expect. There are a lot of questions that could arise during this new experience and learning about the actual flight could help reduce anxiety.
I have heard that you will lose your hearing while taking off, is this true? Why do you need to keep your seatbelts on? Will there be unusual

movements? There could be a lot of questions that could be in the back of your mind. When you find out the answers to each of these questions then you would certainly feel more at ease compared to simply worrying about nothing. Here are some of the most common answers to popular questions that passengers may have:

- No, you will not lose your hearing while the plane is taking off, you will only feel pressure within your ears and this is normal. As the plane moves up, a change in pressure is felt by the sensitive parts of your ear and you may feel some kind of pop but you will still be able to hear.

- You need to keep your seatbelts on while the plane is taking off since the plane is moving fast to be able to take off. You will be allowed to remove your seatbelts once the plane is in the air. You will be asked to place it back once your plane lands or when there is turbulence ahead.

- Unusual movements during a flight are called turbulence. This occurs when a plane flies in an area where there is low pressure to an area with high pressure. Unlike scenes that you see in movies or television shows, turbulence has never caused a commercial airliner to crash. Statistics show that 99% of people that are injured due to turbulence are because they are not wearing their seatbelts as instructed or were hurt because of luggage falling from the top compartment. Turbulence is basically just your car driving on an uneven or rocky road.

2. **Manage your fears by managing your anxieties**

Most people that suffer from aviophobia have higher levels of anxiety compared to most people. By managing your anxieties, you will be able to focus on conquering your fear of flying. There are many tried and tested ways to reduce general anxiety:

- **Control general anxiety through meditation.** Sit still in a quiet room and close your eyes. Rest your back on your chair and place your hands on your lap and both your feet on the floor. Take deep breaths from your nose and then hold for two counts. Exhale through pursed lips. Repeat these steps until you feel relaxed and more composed. As you reach a level of relaxation, picture yourself in a place where you feel calm and safe such as your bedroom, lying on a soft cushion, walking along the beach and so on. Keep this image in your mind. Open your eyes and slowly rise from your chair. Repeat this simple meditation technique every day and each day, try to keep a vivid image on your mind. The more realistic and vivid this image is, the more you will be able to return your thoughts to it in an instant especially when you feel stressed and anxious.

- **Enroll in a yoga class.** If you have time, spend a few days learning yoga. Yoga is the ancient art of strengthening the body's core through a strong mind, body and spirit. Yoga uses movements, poses and breathing to strengthen your body. Engaging in yoga will make you feel relaxed, strong and more in control of your emotions. Practicing yoga every day will definitely help reduce anxiety and help you conquer aviophobia step by step.

- **Consult a professional.** If your anxiety and stress gets the most of you then you should consult a professional to help you. A therapist or a psychiatrist will help find the most suitable treatment for your anxiety. Therapists will usually recommend treatment activities that will help you manage your anxieties such as one on one consultation, group treatments, engaging in treatment activities and other similar strategies. Prescription medication may be provided such as anti-anxiety medications to control moderate to severe anxiety. Medications are usually considered only when other strategies have not improved the patient's condition.

Taking anti-anxiety medications should only be under a professional's recommendation since these could have side effects that could only aggravate anxiety. Always follow your prescription and never alter your dose whatsoever. Any side effect should be automatically reported to your doctor.

- **Taking calming teas will help ease anxiety.** Teas such as those made of lemon and ginger will help reduce stress and anxiety. Take note that each type of tea has its own distinct flavor and taste but all in all these teas are perfect to reduce anxiety:

Chamomile – has a soothing effect and will help you relax and calm down. Chamomile also has a mild sedative effect and is safe to use even for children.

Lemon – has a calming effect that will soothe your mind and your body. The delicious lemony aroma will also help make you feel relaxed and able to fall asleep.

Linden – is a popularly used as teas in areas in Europe because of its mild floral aroma and sweet taste. It can reduce anxiety, induce sleep, control headaches and even help people with indigestion.

Passionflower – drinking passionflower teas will help reduce nervousness and stress plus will even calm you for that good night's sleep.

Valerian root – has a calming and sedative effect and will even help reduce stress to induce sleep. The use of valerian should be controlled since a strong brew could cause headaches, lethargy and stress.

- **A warm bath will help.** Anxiety may be reduced by taking a nice warm bath. Controlling anxiety is essential in reducing aviophobia and by using techniques such as this regularly; you will be able to reduce your anxiety days before your actual flight. Take a nice long soak or bath in warm water. Take time to relax in your bath; dim the lights, place aromatic candles or add drops of aromatic oils in your bath water or play soothing music.

- **Use music to calm you down.** Create a playlist of your favorite music and play this daily to calm you down. As soon as you feel anxious, whip out your earphones and listen to music that you are at home with or music that you can relate to. Play this as you drive, commute, shop or as you run errands. Soon you will be able to control your anxiety even better.

- **Diversion activities.** Divert your attention from your impending flight to other activities that are worthwhile. So instead of sulking and feeling anxious about your fear, why not indulge in sports, hobbies, pastime or other activities that you are interested in. you may indulge in a spa treatment, in your favorite sports or in volunteering to help others. Simple activities like these will eventually help you manage your fears and control your aviophobia for good.

3. **Plan your trip in advance**

You will feel less anxious if you consider the following items in your flight:

- Create your own flight plan by booking weeks in advance if possible. You will be able to choose from a lot of options when you book in advance. For instance, there will surely be more seats available and thus you could pick one that will make you feel less crowded and agitated.

- A seat in an economy class section of a commercial plane could be crowded and may have a lot of factors that could agitate someone that has aviophobia. Children crying, people complaining, crowded seats and low baggage compartments could all contribute to your fear. If you have known about your trip in advance, save money so you can travel first class. First class seats are generally more comfortable, have plenty of leg room, passengers tend to be more refined (and quiet) plus the atmosphere could make you feel more at ease which will certainly contribute to conquering your fear of flying.

Paying for first class seat is of course more expensive compared to traveling in economy but there are airfare promos for different airlines whole year round. You can subscribe to these and get discounts on airfare. If you are travelling abroad, there are more classes to choose from other than economy. You may upgrade to premium economy, business class or subclass or first class.

- A direct flight would be expensive but could be more comfortable and less stressful for you. The sooner you land, the sooner you will feel better. Again avail of discount offers online or offline from your favorite airline so you can travel on a budget.

- If you can pick seats, choose one which is located over the wing. This seat is said to be the most comfortable one in the plane. Again, booking early will help you get the seat you want.

- If you cannot commit to first class travel or business class then choose a seat that will make you feel less trapped. In an economy class, the aisle seat will certainly make you feel at ease or a seat near the exit row.

- Choose an airline that offers great flight features that will make your trip more comfortable for you. Some great entertainment funs are in-flight movies, video games, music and magazines. You may also indulge in snacks or food. You may plan on bringing items or things to do that will make you feel more comfortable such as your own portable gaming console, a music player, a good book to read, some puzzles and so on. The more you are distracted the more you will never feel afraid of flying at all.

- Night time flying could make people with aviophobia more anxious. If you feel this way then by all means book a daytime flight.

- A larger plane technically flies smoother than smaller ones. If you can, choose a larger flight.

- If you are planning for a vacation, schedule your trip during the less crowded seasons of the year. Less people means more opportunities to pick a more comfortable seat, more leg room and certainly less stress since there are a few people complaining, making noise and the like.

- Read online reviews about airline service and pick one that offers a comfortable and less stressful ride. Airlines, especially international flights, are ranked each year and you have the opportunity to pick a flight that will be more convenient for you.

4. Have someone you trust accompany you

If you are travelling on a business, it would be best to go with a group or have someone you trust accompany you during your trip. You will feel less stressed and more at ease when you can talk to someone you know before and during the trip.

5. Visit the airport days before you fly

This is just to help you get acquainted with the terminal and the aircraft. Talk to flight stewardesses or if you could have a chance, you may talk to pilots too.

6. Be early for your flight

During the day of the flight, arrive early. Be sure to be there at least an hour before your scheduled flight so you can have a personal experience with the terminal. Hang around areas where you can see the planes or in places where you can see people moving in and out the terminal area.

Most airports these days are linked to a mall or a place where passengers could shop before their flights. Take your time and relax in these areas so you would be more at ease when you are about to board your flight.

7. Avoid a heavy meal hours before your flight

You will only feel queasy and nauseous when you eat a huge meal. Choose light snacks such as fruits, a salad, a fruit smoothie or a handful of nuts. You can eat a heavy meal later once you have landed.

8. Pack light.

The more you have a lot of luggage the more you need to stress on how these should be handled. If possible, have only a single bag with you where everything you need could be found. Travelling with kids in tow? Have someone that you trust take care of them instead. Focus on yourself and how you can reduce your fears and not on anything else.

During your flight

Even if you feel less anxious, there will surely be a huge possibility that you will experience some agitation as your journey starts. There are some ways to avoid this feeling. Here are some great ways:

1. Avoid caffeine

Avoid drinking drinks with caffeine such as coffee, tea or energy drinks before and during your flight. This will surely agitate you more. Stewardesses will start asking for things that you need as soon as you sit. Ask for a fruity beverage or simply water to refresh you and awaken you.

2. Take to in-flight entertainment

Check the onboard schedule for movies, games or music. Choose the ones that you have been meaning to watch, play or listen to. Any kind of diversion will help get your mind off flying would do.

3. Listen and pay attention to the safety briefing

As soon as every passenger is all accounted for, stewardesses will start their safety briefing. You should listen to this very closely. They will tell you all about the safety measures in the plane and all about where exits could be found. Stewardesses are very friendly and will help you in every way they can.

4. Talk to your seatmate

You will feel at ease if you have someone to talk to. If this is not possible, you may write letters instead. Compose a letter to a friend or a family member to divert your attention.

5. Small distractions will help

There are small but effective ways to divert your attention. Here are some simple but great techniques:
- Place a rubber band or clip on your wrist. Take one end and turn it round and round your wrist. Do this over and over till you feel less anxious. You may also snap this rubber band on your skin to jolt you and divert your attention as well.
- Use a stress ball. Squeeze this ball over and over again to help reduce anxiety.
- Place a small coin in your shoe or any kind of small object that will help distract your attention.
- Read a distracting news article from a magazine to help divert your attention. An outrageous showbiz news, a cheesy romance advice or simply news about anything idiotic will surely help you think less about your flight.

6. Join in-flight activities

Join activities that are led by stewardesses. Usually, there are in-flight BINGOs, karaoke challenges, raffles and talent contests. Joining these fun activities will certainly help reduce your anxiety.

7. Sleep helps

Simply sleeping during the flight will possibly help you buy a lot of time. You may opt to stay awake the night before and sleep during the flight. Of course you should choose a flight that is less crowded and a seat that is in a quiet section of the plane such as the window or at the back. You will only be able to choose seats if you book early too.

After your flight

After your flight, you will surely feel amazing having survived your ordeal! But the treatment to conquer your fears once and for all is not over. You should continue this "recovery" and start living a worry-free life.

1. Think about flying again.

The more you expose yourself to flying, the more you will be able to successfully overcome your fears. Of course you will need to consider flying again especially when you took the plane to get to your destination. Same as what you did the first time.

2. Consider taking up flying lessons.

To make you more at ease with flying, why not fly your own plane? You may take professional flying lessons from a reputable flying school. You can choose from lessons to help you become a professional commercial pilot or simply a course to train you on flying a small plane or a chartered aircraft. These courses take long hours of training as well as patience and focus but this is the ultimate way to completely remove your fear of flying.

3. Take a class that will help you conquer your fears for good.

There are a lot of classes that will unite you with people with the same fears as yours. Your doctor will be able to help recommend the ideal group where you could belong. A class will help you open your heart and your thoughts about your fears with people that have the same experiences as yours. You will learn effective ways to help you conquer your fears for good plus you will also be able to help other people too.

4. Fly more often

There are a lot of opportunities these days to allow you to fly more often through discount coupons, budget seats and low cost airfare. If you fly regularly, you will be able to learn how to conquer your fears and finally be over them for good.

5. Alternative courses

Aside from flying, you can take up other types of activities to address your fears. Some amazing opportunities will be able to help you reduce your fear of flying such as bungee jumping, parachuting from an airplane or from a tall building, paragliding, riding extreme theme park rides and so on.

ALL OR NOTHING

Facing the inevitable

No one could ignore the recent mishaps of different international airlines.

However this does not change the fact that flying is still a very safe mode of transportation.

If you still feel uncomfortable about flying because of recent news, there is no other way but to seek other methods of travel.

However do not close your doors to flying just yet!

Sooner or later, you will be able to let go of your fears and find the courage to try resolving your fears once more.

No one says that this is an easy task but remember this, the sooner you get your fear of flying gone, the faster you will be able to get off and see new places!

Finally, freedom from fear!

Finally, it is time to celebrate!

Your freedom from aviophobia has come!

You are now free from this fear and could take on any other challenge!

You are more likely to enjoy your life when you are able to live without your fear of flying!

Now you can go to different places, live in different countries and maybe tour the world with your fears gone!

Here are some suggestions to try on your next vacation:

- Flight tours to Europe – enjoy a totally out of this world vacation with your loved one to amazing European spots. Tour France, Switzerland, Germany, England and Amsterdam for 10 days. You will be flying via chartered flight to key cities in these countries and visiting amazing tourist spots.

- Flights from Italy with a special emphasis on Lake Maggiore – this is another 10 day tour that starts from Rome to Lake Maggiore in Italy. This amazing experience will let you savor amazing Italian cuisine, meet interesting locals and learn more about different Italian destinations.

- From Vienna to Budapest – this is a combination air and train travel that will take 8 days. Get to enjoy great food, check out amazing tourist spots and meet great people along the way.

Cheers on conquering your fears!

May you have a great time flying around the world!

CONCLUSION

Thank you again for purchasing this book!

I hope this book was able to help you overcome your fear of flying.

I appreciate you for taking the time out of your day or evening to read this book, and if you have an extra second, I would love to hear what you think about this book by leaving a review on Amazon. I would greatly appreciate it!

Now if you want to take your life to the next level and create a life you love then I highly recommend you consider getting this book:

"How to Find Happiness".

This is a cool book and by purchasing a copy you put another copy into the hands of someone less fortunate and help the author on their mission to inspire people to do what they love that also contributes to humanity. That is a win/win/win.

To get this book go to http://amzn.to/1wCl4vc

If the link does not work, for whatever reason, you can simply search for the title "How to Find Happiness" on the Amazon website.

Thank you again, and I wish you nothing but the best!

Giuseppe Formato

Contents from the book "How to Find Happiness"

My Story
Introduction
The Beginning and the End
How to Create a Life You Love
Who Am I Today?
Find My Superpowers
My Past
My Beliefs
Life Phases
Wheel of Life
My Strengths
Which Areas Can I Improve?
What Resources or Help Do I Have Access To?
What Makes Me Happy?
6 Core Human Needs
My Values
What Is My Passion?
Which Road to Take?
My Passion
My Personal Vision Statement
Planning To Live Passionately
10 Reasons Why You Must Set Goals
Guidelines to Goal Setting
Setting My Goals
Time Bound Goals
Area Bound Goals
Prioritizing My Goals
Making My Goals SMARTER
My Life Plan on a Page
Milestones
Actions and Tasks
Goal Achievement Plan
My Weekly Timetable
Things To Do Today
Living Passionately
14 Reasons Why People Do Not Achieve Their Goals
Motivation and Focus
Coach Yourself to Success
What is Success?
Thankful List
Morning Success Ritual

Evening Success Ritual
Pain and Pleasure
Dealing with Change
Stress Reduction
Changing My Negative Self-Talk or Self-Limiting beliefs
Cognitive Behavioral Approach
Neuro-linguistic programming (NLP)
Solution Focused Approach
Narrative Approach
Which Coaching Approach to Use
Improving Your Relationships
Dealing with a Problem
Conclusion

To get this book go to http://amzn.to/1wCl4vc

If the link does not work, for whatever reason, you can simply search for the title "How to Find Happiness" on the Amazon website.

Printed in Poland
by Amazon Fulfillment
Poland Sp. z o.o., Wrocław